# My Mess

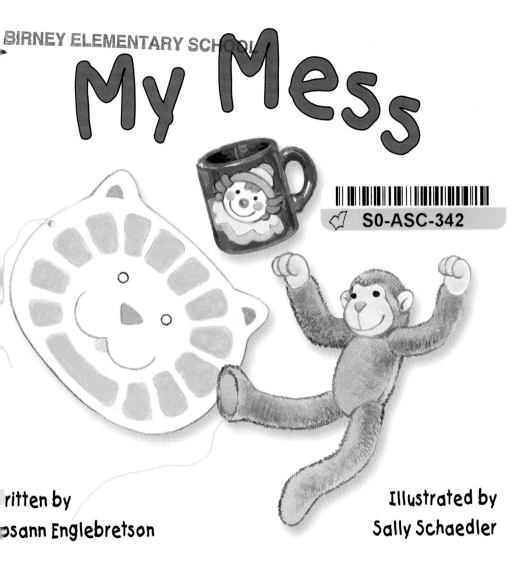

Written by
Rosann Englebretson

Illustrated by
Sally Schaedler

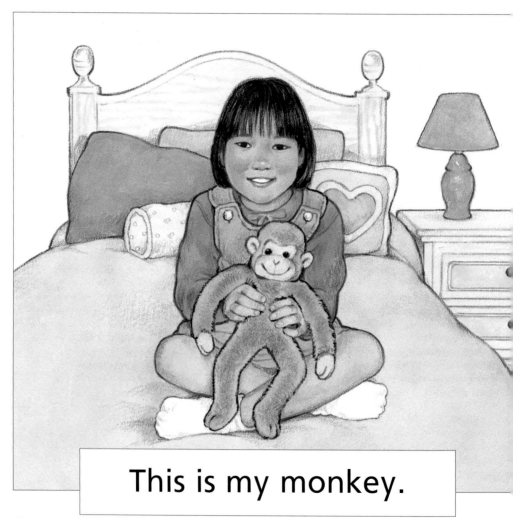

This is my monkey.

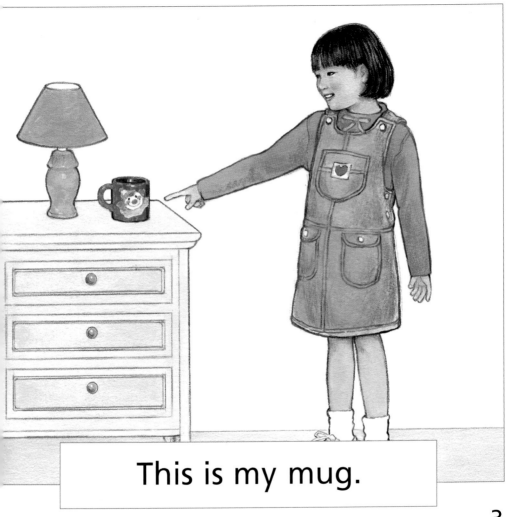

This is my mug.

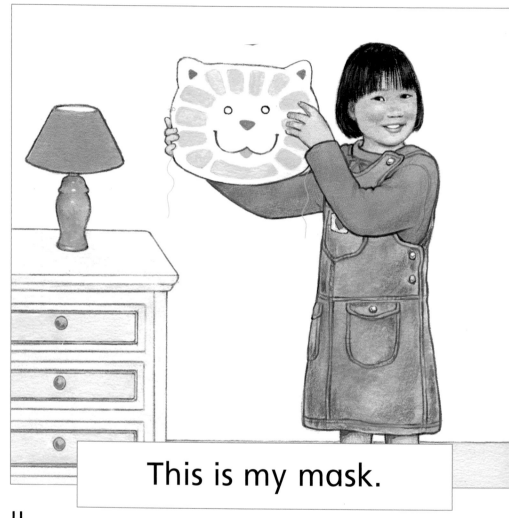

This is my mask.

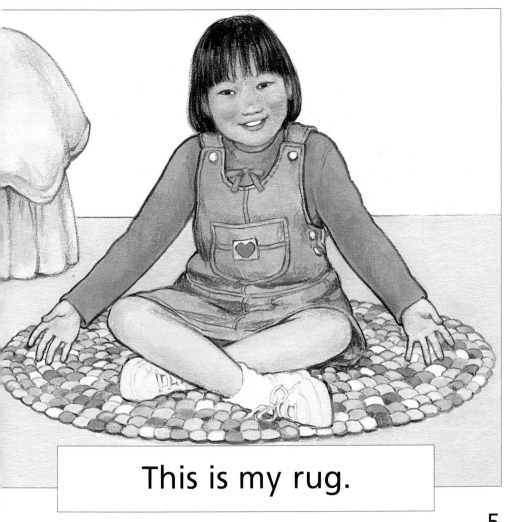

This is my rug.

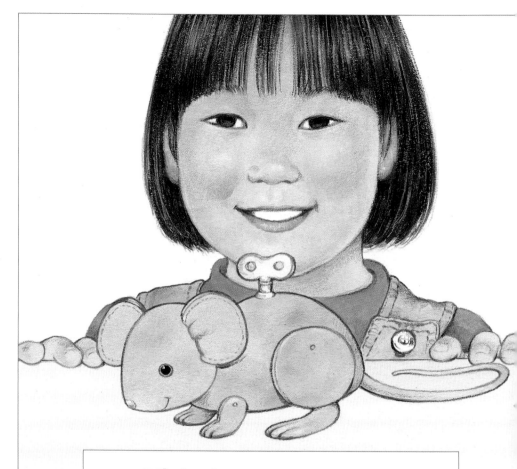

This is my mouse.

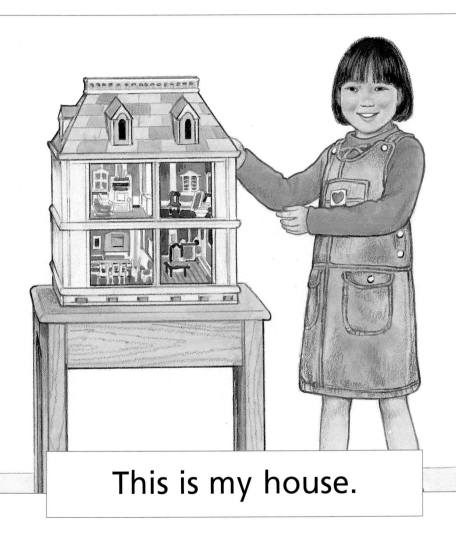

This is my house.

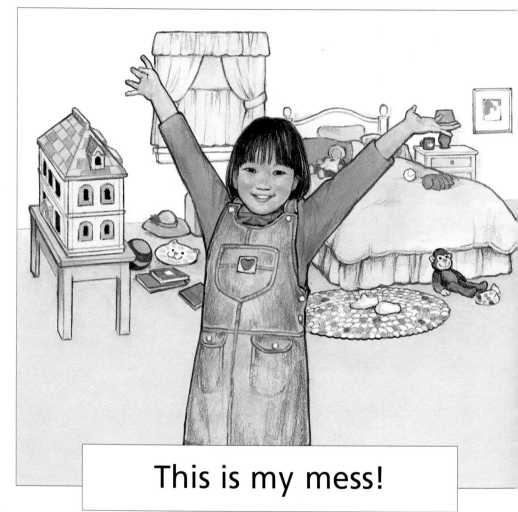

This is my mess!